Syrups and Cordials

HOW THEY USED TO DO IT

Copyright © 2013 Two Magpies Publishing

An imprint of Read Publishing Ltd
Home Farm, 44 Evesham Road,
Cookhill, Alcester,
Warwickshire, B49 5LJ

Commissioning Editor Rose Hewlett
Written by Amelia Carruthers
Design by Zoë Horn Haywood

All Images remain the copyright property of their respective owners, all attributions and copyright licences are referenced at the rear of the book.

This book is copyright and may not be reproduced or copied in any way without the express permission of the publisher in writing.

British Library Cataloguing-in-Publication Data.
A catalogue record for this book is available from the British Library.

Contents

Introduction 3

Cordials: A History 9

The Story of the Store Cupboard 13
    Staple Ingredients 16

Sourcing Your Supplies 21

Equipment and Preparation 25

Measurements 29

Essential Skills.......................... 35

Recipes 39
    Elderflower Cordial.................... 42
    Highland Cordial 48
    Lemon Syrup 52
    Quince Syrup 56
    Blackberry Cordial 62
    Cherry Syrup 66
    Strawberry Syrup 70
    Raspberry Syrup 74
    Blackcurrant and....................... 78
    Blackcurrant and Liquorice Cordial 78
    Liquorice Cordial 78
    Blood Orange Syrup..................... 84
    Plum Syrup............................. 88

Contents

    Pineapple Syrup 92
    Apricock Syrup 96
    Lavender Syrup 102
    Rose Syrup 106
    Rose Petals 110
    Violet Syrup 112
    Lovage Cordial 116
    Aniseed Cordial 122
    Cinnamon Cordial 126
    Juniper Cordial 130
    Clove Cordial 134
    Cranberry Syrup 140
    Dandelion Cordial 144
    Ginger Syrup 148
    Rosehip Cordial 152

Serving Suggestions 157

Gorgeous Gifts 163

'SOME BOOKS ARE TO BE TASTED, OTHERS TO BE SWALLOWED, AND SOME FEW TO BE CHEWED AND DIGESTED.'

Francis Bacon

Foreword

The simple pleasure of mastering practical household skills has been all but forgotten over the last century. We live in an overly convenient, disposable world in which things arrive pre-packed, ready-wrapped and lacking in any craft, care, or quality.

It's time to reject this attrition of what were once everyday skills, time to get back to basics, time to remember How They Used To Do It! The 'How They Used To Do It' series will take you back to the golden age of practical skills; an age where making and mending, cooking and preserving, brewing and bottling, were all done within the home. This fun, and proudly *kitsch* series will instruct you in a whole range of traditional skills that have fallen out of use, putting old knowledge into new hands. Using household items, nifty hints and tricks, and a little creativity you will be surprised what you can achieve.

The series has been carefully curated from a wealth of original resources to provide a wonderful blend of social history and practical instruction. The knowledge within these pages has been sourced from rare books, old newspapers and forgotten magazines to inform a whole new generation about *How They Used To Do It*.

Introduction

Introduction

WELCOME TO THE WONDERFUL WORLD OF SYRUPS AND CORDIALS

Introduction

The main benefit of homemade cordials and syrups is that *you* can pick the best and purest ingredients yourself. In an increasingly synthetic age, knowing exactly what has gone into your lovingly created beverages is a rare luxury. With just a little time, effort and outlay, the end result is incredibly rewarding!

Herein lies the philosophy behind the 'How They Used To Do It' series. With this little book in your hands you can turn a humble kitchen into a hub of drink-making activity, happily passing many a rainy (or sunny!) day creating delicious and refreshing concoctions. As well as lots of classic recipes, this book is filled with tips and techniques on making the perfect syrups or cordials. What's more, you don't even need lots of equipment or a vast array of ingredients to get started.

Introduction

Making your own cordials at home is very often cheaper than buying them - perfect for the thrifty home-chef. The cost of ingredients is low (especially if you pick them yourself), and by creating large batches of cordials and syrups, you can save a huge amount of money. It is *incredibly easy* to make syrups and cordials at home. Essentially the process involves steeping or cooking your chosen ingredients in liquids – waiting – straining – and then consuming! Cordials also have an incredibly long history; they are the descendants of herbal medicines, made in Italy as early as the thirteenth century and were often prepared by monks and other healers. Nowadays, syrups and cordials are made worldwide and served in many ways: by themselves, poured over ice or ice-cream, with cocktails or with any manner of dessert. Some are prepared by infusing certain woods, fruits or flowers in water, and adding sugar or other items, and yet others are distilled from aromatics.

Introduction

To make a syrup or cordial, the preliminary ingredients are usually cooked, be it spices, vanilla, flowers, caramel, peppermint, fruits, coffee…etc. with a basic syrup, consisting of roughly equal amounts of sugar and water. The mix is then brought to the boil, simmered for a further twelve to twenty minutes and taken off the heat. It is then strained if necessary. This rough guide will of course change from recipe to recipe, though it is a good place to start. The wonderful thing about making your own homemade products is the fun one can have with creating customised labels and garnishes to the finished bottles (think berries, citrus zest, herb sprigs) – a perfect vintage-inspired present as well as personal treat. We hope that the reader is inspired by this book to start making their own syrups and cordials, a delicious, historical, as well as rewarding pastime. Enjoy.

Amelia Carruthers

Introduction

"I have confined myself exclusively to homemade beverages, gathering my fruits and flowers from old-fashioned, homely gardens. I leave to your imagination the times, fashions, and customs they recall. The aroma that clings to them is subtle. Age has blended and mellowed all that was crude in those bygone days.

With a gentle hand I tie my little bunch together and present you with my bouquet…."

Helen Saunders Wright,
Old Time Recipes for Homemade Wines,
Cordials and Liqueurs *(1909)*

Cordials: A History

Cordials: A History

"Hope is the cordial that keeps life from stagnating."

Samuel Richardson

Cordials and syrups were originally enjoyed in Renaissance Italy. In this period of great cultural change and achievement, which lasted from the fourteenth to the sixteenth century, they were used as tonics and early medicines.

A 'cordial' in its truest sense is any invigorating and stimulating preparation, intended for medicinal purposes. Many early cordials were believed to be especially beneficial to the heart (*cor* in Latin). Many were also considered aphrodisiacs, a view which encouraged their consumption in a social as opposed to a medical context. Other early varieties

Cordials: A History

of alcoholic cordials were flavoured with spices and herbal ingredients, thought to settle the stomach after excessive eating. Popular mixtures included *Rosa Solis*, made in Turin from the sundew plant – thought to invigorate the heart. *Royal Usquebaugh* is an example of a cordial thought to aid digestion, containing flecks of gold leaf, aniseed, liquorice and saffron, sweetened with fruit sugar of figs and raisins. Not one for everyday drinking!

Most syrups and cordials appeared independently. Although first produced in Italian apothecaries during the Renaissance (where they had refined the art of distilling), they were very soon after found in France, referred to as *Liqueurs d'Italie*. This is also where we get the term 'liqueur' from. The first

Cordials: A History

cordials and syrups arrived in England as late as the fifteenth century, and were called 'distilled cordial waters.' These were generally alcoholic medicines, prescribed in small doses to invigorate the heart, body and spirit. It was only in the eighteenth century that people across Europe started making cordials and syrups for recreational consumption though, probably influenced by the lessening of the 'sugar tax' in 1874. During the austerity years of the early twentieth century, the 'make-do-and-mend' ethic really came into its own, and the real benefits of homemade syrups and cordials were witnessed. They allowed people to cheaply and conveniently collect ingredients (often from their own gardens, parks and hedgerows), transform, use - and importantly, *store* them. Nowadays, cordials and syrups are especially popular in Western Europe, with many homemade as well as shop-bought varieties, but less so in countries such as America.

The Story of the Store Cupboard

The Story of the Store Cupboard

Kitchens have come an awfully long way in the past century, as have the supplies stocked in pantries and larders. Before modern conveniences such as fridges and freezers, one of the biggest hurdles housewives had to overcome was the task of preserving, and it was no mean feat! It is hard to imagine a world without the convenience of modern kitchen appliances, and keeping food fresh was a daily challenge.

There are many simple preservation methods that can be carried out in the kitchen, without the use of modern conveniences. Salt can be used to cure meat and fish, and pickling can preserve vegetables. The drying of fruit, herbs and spices is especially useful, and can be used across a wide range of recipes including sweets. Luckily, syrups and cordials are also perfect preservation methods!

Sugar is a natural preservative meaning it could be used by housewives alongside some clever cooking to preserve a glut

The Story of the Store Cupboard

of seasonal produce or expensive fruits. Having a well-stocked larder was the mark of a good housewife, and before easy preservation and storage methods became commonplace, homemade syrups and cordials were *de-rigueur*. Lessening food waste is a thoroughly worthwhile project (both *then* and *now*). During the autumn months especially, when certain fruits are in abundance, making batches of cordials and syrups to store is a great way of ensuring none of the delicious fruits are wasted. Although the drinks-makers of the past would not have had this option, your homemade beverages can be stored in the fridge (or freezer) for many months, allowing you to enjoy your hard work throughout the winter months.

STAPLE INGREDIENTS

When making cordials and syrups - there aren't many! All you will need to source is a good quantity of sugar, water, and whatever 'main flavour' you decide upon. Thankfully, water in the UK is (and was) readily abundant to all, and if the fruits and flowers to go in your concoctions are grown or foraged - sugar really is the only essential you will need to buy. Here, it is worthwhile taking a little time to get to know this basic, but highly important ingredient:

"I seek constantly to improve my manners and graces, for they are the sugar to which all are attracted."

Og Mandino

The Story of the Store Cupboard

Sugar

These days, sugar is a staple ingredient - found in almost all pantries across the country. It is readily available in many different forms; granulated, caster, demerara, muscovado… etc., the list goes on! Go back one hundred, or even fifty years though, and this most certainly would not have been the case.

The history of sugar is, of course, inextricably linked with the history of slavery - and Britain as a large colonial power had a large part to play in this human exploitation. Before the seventeenth century, in Britain and throughout most of Europe, honey was the main ingredient used to sweeten foods. But after Britain took Jamaica and other parts of the West Indies from Spain in 1655, this changed. By 1750 there

The Story of the Store Cupboard

were 120 British refining factories, producing 30,000 tonnes of sugar a year from sugar cane. Sugar was heavily taxed though and it was not until 1874 that this levy was removed and sugar became more affordable.

Until the late nineteenth century, sugar came in the form of 'sugarloaf' which was essentially a hard bloc of the raw material. Housewives would buy their sugar in tall, conical loaves, and trim off what they needed with special iron sugar-cutters called sugar nips. If a recipe called for fine, granulated sugar, then a little elbow grease and a pestle and mortar would be enthusiastically employed! Whilst granulated sugar was not far behind, the two World Wars put the brakes on the nation's sugar consumption. It was among the first items to be rationed in 1918, alongside butter, margarine, lard and meat.

The Story of the Store Cupboard

During the 1930s, the country's love affair with sugar came under attack. As World War II air raid sirens sounded throughout Britain's cities, a different war was being fought behind closed doors. Trade routes to the UK were targeted during the war, and food supplies quickly dwindled. On 8th January 1940, bacon, butter and sugar were rationed by the government, followed in subsequent months by meat, tea, jam and much more.

Despite being armed with her government-issued ration book, the average housewife's weekly shopping basket was suddenly much lighter than before. Creating tasty and nutritious meals for the family became a real challenge for many. Sugar became a very precious resource, and a thriving black market quickly sprung up as a result of the strict rationing. With legitimate supplies so very low, mothers had to be increasingly inventive in order to supply their children

The Story of the Store Cupboard

and husbands with sweet treats. To give you a picture of 'how they used to do it' in the 1940s - The average allowance of sugar was 8 oz (227g) a week.

Sourcing Your Supplies

Sourcing Your Supplies

These days, we are incredibly lucky to be sure of a well stocked pantry. Without the convenience of large supermarkets, it could take a busy housewife the best part of the day to fill her shopping basket with supplies for the week from her local high street.

Making your own cordials and syrups is a fantastic way to use up surplus produce, much of which you may have grown yourself, or naturally foraged. Work out when fruits are in abundance, what time of year is best to pick them, and most importantly, *where* you can find them. In June, elderflowers are just coming out, whilst in July the blackcurrants make an appearance, followed by plums in September. For the more exotic cordial or syrup though, as well as for necessary ingredients such as lemons, your local food-store should have everything you need.

Sourcing Your Supplies

An important question to bear in mind when choosing your ingredients, is - does it have enough flavour when cooked to bear being diluted? Mellow fruits like apples for example, make a wonderfully fresh juice, but once you boil them - adding sugar and water, this will just be a tasteless sugary drink. Crab Apples, Quince and Rosehips have similar, 'earthy' flavours, and make good alternatives to the standard apple. As a rule of thumb, if you could happily eat large quantities of the fruit or other 'main ingredient' in question, then it will probably not make a very good finished cordial.

Finding the best ingredients before you put your apron on and start cooking is important, as the lovelier your ingredients are, the lovelier your drinks will be. Look at the local produce on offer in your area. It is so often the case that the best things to eat are the things that grow locally, are in season, and haven't travelled a huge distance. Not only do

Sourcing Your Supplies

these things taste better than their imported counterparts, but it is far kinder to the environment to use what is nearby. Perhaps you have a wonderful local greengrocer who can supply you with seasonal fruit, or a brilliant local health food shop where you can stock up on herbs and spices? Use your local suppliers and their expertise, as their knowledge will be rather useful to you while you are still getting to grips with the basics.

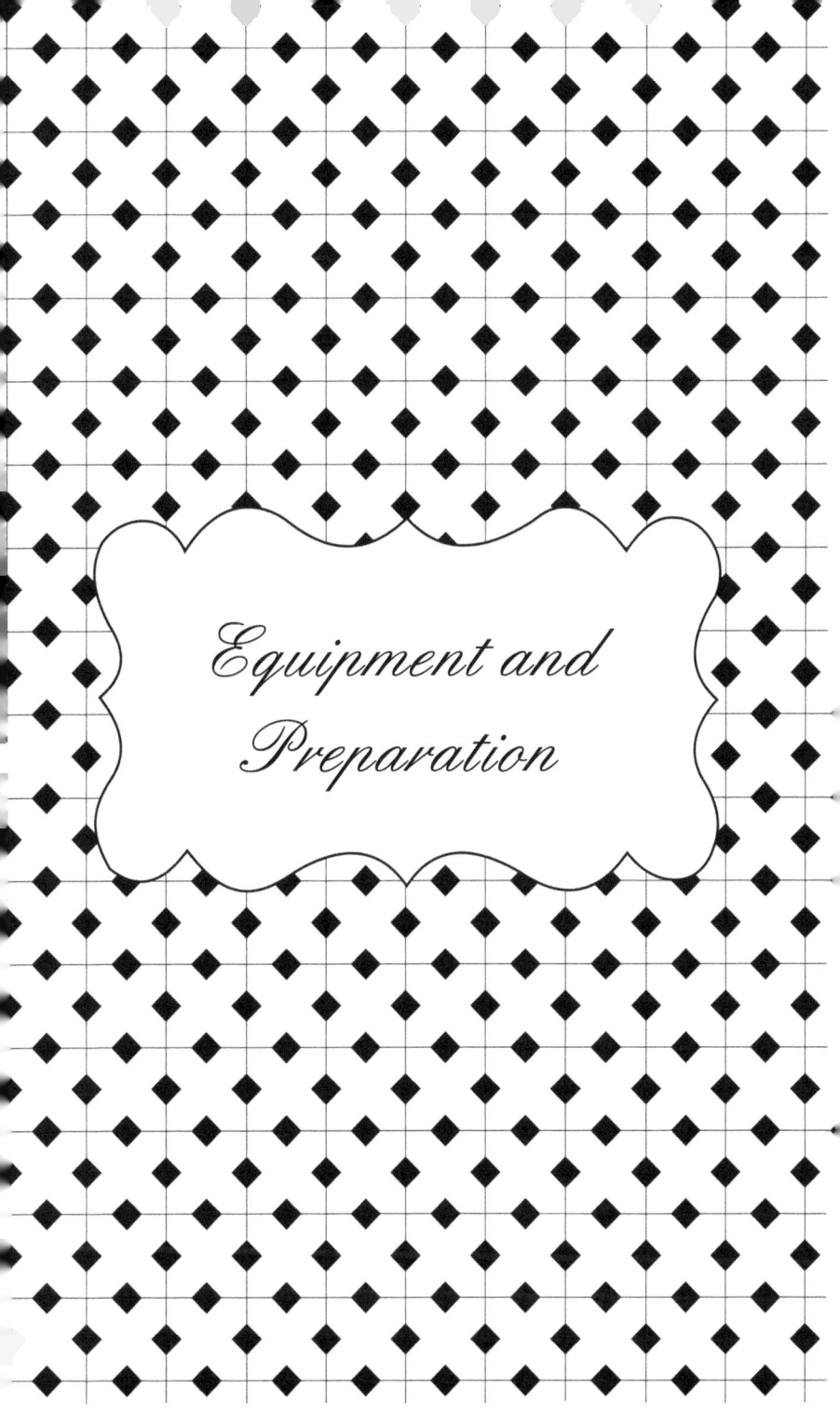

Equipment and Preparation

Equipment and Preparation

Now you have stocked your store cupboard, let's have a look at the kitchen equipment you will need to find before getting started on your first batch syrups or cordials. The list of utensils and equipment you will need is not huge, but it is important you have the basics at your fingertips. Your kitchen utensils are the tools of your trade, as it were, and you'll get the best results from your beverage making if you take the time to source the right tools.

The equipment needed for cordial and syrup making is rather basic, and you may already have most of it around the house. You will need saucepans, any earthenware or non-porous bowls and either glass or plastic bottles (size and amount dependent on the batch size you are intending), as well as material (usually muslin) for straining. When you have cooked the ingredients in a saucepan (heavy bottomed jam boilers work best), you may find it useful to purchase a stand or tripod, from which to leave the mixture to strain

Equipment and Preparation

overnight. This is by no means necessary though, and a sieve and wooden spoon would work just as well for smaller batches! Although the types of saucepans, bowls and bottles you will need to make cordials with are not difficult to find, it is important that you take the time to get your equipment ready before you start making your first batch.

Always ensure the fruits that you use in your syrup or cordial recipes have been washed thoroughly, especially if they have been gathered from low hedgerows, or bushes that are near roads. If the fruits have pips or cores, you may wish to remove these before cooking, as some may leave a bitter taste to the final product. Some however, such as rosehips are perfectly fine to add whole; just remember to strain thoroughly before the final stages…

All the recipes in this book will use roughly 500g of fruit (if this is the main ingredient), which should produce roughly 700ml of syrup / cordial. The amount of syrup and cordial you

Equipment and Preparation

produce will depend on how strong you wish the end result to be. Some people prefer much thicker, viscous syrups, whilst others will only be looking for a lightly flavoured cordial. Other ingredients such as lavender, cinnamon, aniseed or ginger will require less 'primary ingredient' though, as their natural flavours are so strong. Have fun experimenting and just use what you've got!

Measurements

Measurements

"Haste still pays haste, and leisure answers leisure;
Like doth quit like, and Measure still for Measure."

***Shakespeare**, Measure for Measure*

Here, we were in a dilemma!

Of course, in the 'golden-age' of home cooking, measurements would have been very rough; using simple ratios was the most common practice. i.e. 'one part water to one part sugar' and so on. Others would have utilised kitchen cups (which, pre-1890s could have been any size!), and yet other cordial makers, as we move into the twentieth century, would have started using ounces, pounds and pints.

Cups have been used in cookery for generations, their use gained in popularity after an American culinary expert

Measurements

called Fanny Farmer introduced them as a standardised form of measurement in recipes. Her emphasis on accuracy and consistency in recipes was groundbreaking for the time, and has since sparked a revolution in the way we cook. Fanny published her best-known cookery book 'The Boston Cooking-School Cook Book' in 1896, in which she stressed the importance of levelling off the cup as you measure. This may seem insignificant, but before her clever intervention, cooks had to make do with instructions such as 'a large dash', 'a goodly pinch', and even 'butter the size of an egg'. Rather amusing, but a little inconsistent, don't you agree?

Now we are of course aware, that most of our readers will not possess standardised 'chefs cups', and nor may they be

Measurements

au-fait with the exact quantities of a 'goodly pinch.' For this reason, we decided to update all the old recipes into grams; leaving the traditional ingredients and methods - but just making life a little easier for the modern cook.

If you do wish for complete historical accuracy, we have included a handy table for converting grams to ounces to cups, and likewise cups to pints to milliliters. Whether you prefer to don the traditional cup, frilly pinafore and wooden spoon, or take a more updated approach to the classics - we leave the choice up to you…

Measurements

'Cups to Classics' - Conversion Chart

Water	1 Cup	8 Fluid oz	½ Pint	237 ml
Sugar	1 Cup	4.5 oz	n/a	200g
	1 Tablespoon	0.89 oz	n/a	12g

To summarise...

1 cup = 4.5 ounces
1 ounce = 28.34 grams
1 pound = 0.453 kilograms
1 gram = 0.035 ounces
1 kilogram = 2.2 pounds
1 Fluid oz = 29.57 milliliters.

Measurements

More handy weight conversions:

1 Tablespoon = 5 Fluid oz, or 14.79 ml
3 Teaspoons = 1 Tablespoon
4 Tablespoons = ¼ Cup
16 Tablespoons = 1 Cup

Essential Skills

Essential Skills

There really is only one key skill the would-be cordial or syrup maker will have to master: Filtering. This technique though, is done in exactly the same way, using exactly the same materials (that is cotton or muslin cloth) as it always has been. - Some things just can't be improved upon!

Filtering through material is a much easier way of improving your beverages than using 'burnt alum', 'the white of eggs' or 'isinglass' for purification. It is an easy but essential technique to master, and can be done in a number of ways. Pouring your cordial or syrup through a clean muslin cloth, or (if you're cheating 'the modern way'), a funnel lined with coffee filter paper, is a simple process which will really add to the quality of your finished beverage. This should hopefully remove any sediment. Here, try to avoid (if possible) actively pushing the mixture through the cloth or paper; as this will result in a slightly cloudier end result.

Essential Skills

Depending on how much syrup or cordial you have made, filtering may be a two person job! This is great, as cooking has always been a communal activity, traditionally used as the perfect bonding activity for the female members of the household. If you only have a little liquid, pouring it through a lined funnel will suffice. However if you have doubled or even tripled our recipies, asking a friend to help you keep the muslin taught over a large bowl or bucket will be an invaluable help! For the more dedicated syrup and cordial maker, you may also consider buying a tripod, from which to hang the filtering material. On your own or with a friend, it's important to get this right.

Some recipes may call for you to filter the liquid a number of times and some may not need filtering at all. Recipes differ greatly, so make sure you read the method instructions carefully before starting work on your first batch.

Essential Skills

Traditional Favourites

"Vulgar curiosity made me bold to inquire the names of a few… imagine my astonishment when they [the ladies of the village] graciously told that the gay dandelion, the modest daisy, the blushing currant, had one and all contributed their nectar to the joy of the occasion. Flattered by my interest, my gentle hostess broke strict rules of etiquette and invited me to linger, showing me rare old gardens aglow with flowers, fruits and vegetables that in due time would contribute to their store, and at parting various time-worn recipes were urged upon me, with verbal instructions and injunctions upon the best methods of putting them to test."

Helen Saunders Wright, Old Time Recipes for Homemade Wines, Cordials and Liqueurs *(1909)*

ELDERFLOWER CORDIAL

Seven long strides shalt thou take,
And if Long Compton thou canst see
King of England thou shalt be…
As Long Compton thou canst not see
King of England thou shalt not be.
Rise up stick and stand still stone
For King of England thou shalt be none.
Thou and thy men bleak stones shall be,
And I myself an eldern tree…

This is the tale of how the Rollright Stones, that lie on the border between Oxfordshire and Warwickshire came to be. When the king and his knights marched towards a

Elderflower Cordial

town called Long Compton, they came upon a witch (the Elder Mother) who recanted the lines above... The King purposefully strode towards his goal, but on his seventh stride, a hill rose up before Long Compton making him unable to see the town. And thus the King and his knights were turned to stone and the witch turned herself into an elder tree...

The Elder Mother is thought to be the guardian of the elder trees, and it's been said in English folklore that you must ask the Elder Mother's permission before taking any wood from the elder tree, or else ill luck will befall you. So be extra careful when picking her flowers, not to end up like this unfortunate King! Elderflowers are, of course, the pretty white flowers of the elder tree. They have been used to make beverages for centuries, appearing in abundance in the British hedgerows - and are believed to have a number of

Elderflower Cordial

health benefits. There is a whole host of wonderful folklore surrounding this lovely tree, one such tale recounting that the most auspicious time to encounter faeries is underneath the elder on midsummer night's eve. Its still an important plant today, and one of the main health benefits of eldcrflowers are that they are antioxidants, cleansing the lymph glands and reducing susceptibility to many chronic (mostly age-related) conditions. Our forebears already knew this; and used elder to protect from rheumatism.

Elderflowers are best gathered on a warm day (never when wet), just as the many tiny buds are beginning to open. Do

Elderflower Cordial

remember to leave some flowers for elderberry picking later in the year though. This recipe for elderflower cordial is sweet yet subtly flavoured, and has a gentle, floral aroma; perfect as an 'afternoon accompaniment.' In true *How They Used To Do It* style, it can also be used as a great base for a fresh fruit salad or to make a stunning sorbet - nothing will go to waste! For the adventurous cordial-maker, pink grapefruit would also make a lovely foil its delicate flavour. Try garnishing with some of the pretty little flowers themselves for a truly elegant finish.

Elderflower Cordial

About 25 Elderflower Heads

3 Lemons

1 Orange

1kg sugar

1 heaped tsp. citric acid (optional)

1.5 litres of Water

Elderflower Cordial

1. Carefully inspect the elderflower heads, making sure to remove any insects. Place them in a large bowl. **2.** Zest and juice the lemons and orange, and put this in the bowl with the elderflower. Add the sugar and the citric acid too. **3.** Bring 1.5 litres of water to the boil, and pour it over the flowers and zest. Stir. **4.** Cover overnight and leave to infuse. It is up to you how long you leave the mixture for – some only do this for a day, others for a week. The longer you leave it, the better the flavour, just make sure to stir it each day. Don't go much over a week though. **5.** Strain the liquid through a piece of muslin. **6.** Using a funnel, pour the liquid into sterilised bottles. Your cordial is ready to serve!

HIGHLAND CORDIAL

If Heaven a draught of heavenly pleasure spare,
One cordial in this melancholy vale,
'T is when a youthful, loving, modest pair
In other's arms breathe out the tender tale.
Robert Burns, The Cotter's Saturday Night

This traditional Scottish recipe for 'Highland cordial' uses a little ginger and a lot of lemon zest for a really zingy, punchy flavour. The white-currants, ginger and lemon will impart a refreshing sourness to the drink, counteracted with generous amounts of sugar. White-currants are also perfect for

Highland Cordial

old-fashioned-foraging because they are just as sweet and delightful as their red and black cousins, but aren't as attractive to birds because of their pale hue. Make up a jug of it with iced water to serve to guests as a really unusual and delicious non-alcoholic cocktail.

If you are getting truly in the 'highland spirit' this beverage used to be made with generous amounts of whisky replacing the water; usually an entire bottle. Perfect for warming your cockles round a blazing fire! The finely curled lemon peel would make a lovely garnish when serving.

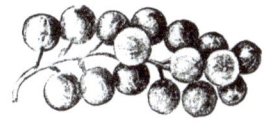

Highland Cordial

500g White Currants
350ml boiling Water
1 teaspoon Ginger essence
1 Lemon (peeled rind)
300g Sugar

Highland Cordial

1. Place the currants into a large jar or bowl and pour the boiling water over them. **2.** Cover with a clean cloth and leave to stand until cool. **3.** Pour the mixture into a heavy-bottomed saucepan with the sugar, lemon rind and ginger and boil for ten minutes. **4.** Strain the mixture through a clean muslin cloth and pour into sterilised bottles to store. The longer you store this liquid, the better it will taste. Traditional recipes advise anything up to three months.

LEMON SYRUP

Lemons…

This fascinating ingredient really deserves an entire section itself! Lemons have been used in British domestic kitchens for longer than you may think… The first substantial cultivation of lemons in Europe began in Genoa in the middle of the fifteenth century. The lemon was later introduced to the Americas and beyond in 1493 when Christopher Columbus brought them along on his voyages. It has been a revolution to the humble-home cook ever since!

Citrus fruits make wonderful-tasting syrups, and this one will also have the most gorgeous, vibrant colour thanks to the lemon's natural hue. This recipe for lemon syrup is a classic

Lemon Syrup

recipe to master. Once you have a supply of lemon syrup, you will amazed at how many uses you will find for it. Not only can it be diluted and enjoyed as a soft drink, but it is a really quick and easy way of adding an extra citrus tang to mixed cocktails at home. This recipe uses the juice, zest and rinds - really making the most of this wonderful fruit. Lemon syrup is also incredibly handy if you are making a lemon drizzle cake, or for that matter – any other lemon based dish (sweet or savoury).

Lemon Syrup

12 Lemons
500g Sugar
225ml Water

Lemon Syrup

1. Juice the lemons, but make sure to keep six of the rinds too. **2.** Rub sugar onto the rinds of the six lemons and place into a large heavy-bottomed saucepan with the water. **3.** Boil the mixture until clear, and then add all the strained lemon juice. **4.** Simmer gently for five minutes. **5.** Strain the mixture through a clean muslin cloth (optional). **6.** Pour into sterilised bottles and seal. Garnish with curls of peeled lemon zest (optional!) **7.** Store in the fridge or freezer, or use straight away.

QUINCE SYRUP

"They dined on mince, and slices of quince, Which they ate with a runcible spoon; And hand in hand, on the edge of the sand, They danced by the light of the moon."

Edward Lear

Quince Charming: Quince are small fruits which belong to the same family as pears - and a much under-used and under-appreciated British fruit. Quince trees were first recorded in Britain in 1275, when Edward I planted four at the Tower of London. They may have arrived earlier though, as thirteenth century English recipes included pie-crusts filled with whole quinces coated in honey and sprinkled with ginger

Quince Syrup

(Delicious). Gradually though, apples and pears edged them out of culinary favour - but now, the Quince is making a come back!

They are grown all over England now, and are a treat to find. Pick them in October or November, leaving to ripen in a cool place if necessary. Quince trees are often grown for their pretty pink flowers, but the fruits can be used in jams and preserves, as well as this simple and straightforward recipe for quince syrup. Quince has an earthy flavour, almost a cross between an apple and a pear, and is commonly used as an accompaniment to cheese.

When hosting a dinner party, why not try this syrup as an after dinner aperitif (alongside your cheese course)? You will truly be the hostess with the mostess with this!

Quince Syrup

500g fresh, ripe Quinces
200g Sugar
Dash of Water
1 Lemon

Quince Syrup

1. Put the (cut up) quinces, sugar and water in a saucepan, and bring to the boil. **2.** Reduce the heat and place a slightly smaller lid over the fruit to keep it submerged. **3.** Simmer until the liquid is pale pink and has been reduced to a thin syrup. This will usually take about an hour. **4.** Strain the mixture through a clean cloth, and reserve the cooked quines to make some delicious stuffing with. **5.** Stir in the lemon juice. **6.** Your syrup is ready to serve.

British Berries

"Having procured berries that are fully ripe, put them into a tub or pan with a tap to it, and pour upon them as much boiling water as will just cover them. As soon as the heat will permit the hand to be put into the vessel, bruise them well till all the berries are broke. Then let them stand covered till the berries begin to rise toward the top, which they usually do in three or four days... to every ten quarts of this liquid [add] four pounds of sugar."

Pierre Lacour, The Manufacture of Liquors, Wines, and Cordials, Without the Aid of Distillation *(1863)*

Blackberry Cordial

BLACKBERRY CORDIAL

Blackberries are wonderful little fruits, found all over England, most often growing wild in hedgerows. During the autumn months they are in abundance, so why not gather some up to make this delicious fruit cordial. This would have been the perfect drink in times of austerity, easy to find and quick to make… Make sure you rinse the fruit thoroughly before you get started.

It should be noted that these amounts are used for guidance purposes only; in general just utilise however many berries (or other fruits) you have picked, and add sugar according to your own tastes. This is how they would have used to do it

Blackberry Cordial

after all! Cordial making is a fun, and highly personalised business – so get creative.

Blackberry Cordial

500g Blackberries
Cold Water (to cover)
150g Caster Sugar
1 Cinnamon stick
1 Lemon

Blackberry Cordial

1. Take your (washed) berries and place them in a large saucepan. **2.** Pour over the boiling water and cook until the berries start to release their juice. You can mash the berries to aid this juice extraction. **3.** Strain off the berries through a clean muslin cloth. **4**. Add the sugar, lemon juice and cinnamon (again, to taste) and boil for around fifteen minutes (or until the sugar has completely dissolved), skimming off any scum. **5.** Carefully bottle the cordial, seal and store in the fridge.

Cherry Syrup

CHERRY SYRUP

"Four quarts of wild cherries stemmed and well washed, four quarts water. (I put mine in a big yellow bow, and cover with double cheese-cloth, and set behind the kitchen stove…) Then strain, and add three-quarters pound sugar to each quart of liquid."

Cherries and syrups are a match made in heaven! The sweet flavour and vibrant colour of these little stone fruits make them the perfect fruit to use as a base in a syrup. The juice of cherries is wonderfully sweet and slightly syrupy in consistency, lending itself perfectly to this recipe. Cherries are in season during July in the UK, so this is a great recipe to try in the summer. Try adding the syrup to champagne,

Cherry Syrup

for a cherry bellini - perfect for whiling away those balmy (we hope!) british evenings.

For a more unusual twist, why not add hibiscus flowers to your syrup? This will give a rich, crimson colouring and a tart, cranberry-like flavour to the drink. Make sure to add some fresh flowers as a colourful garnish to really impress your guests...

Cherry Syrup

500g Cherries
100g Sugar
10g Cornflour
1 Cinnamon stick
A dash of Water

Cherry Syrup

1. Put the cornflour, water and sugar in a pan – cooking at a low heat until it forms a runny paste. **2.** Add the cherries and the cinnamon to the pan, adding a little more water if required. **3.** Cook the cherries for about twenty minutes. **4.** It is (as usual) up to you, whether you strain the cherry fruits at this point, or keep them in the syrup. **5.** Allow the mixture to cool, then carefully pour into sterilised bottles or jars.

Strawberry Syrup

STRAWBERRY SYRUP

"One must ask the children and birds how cherries and strawberries taste."

Johann Wolfgang von Goethe

Here is a really simple recipe for a sweet and vibrant-coloured syrup. Scottish strawberries are especially famed for their wonderful taste, the colder climate doing these little fruits wonders. Housewives up and down the country could have planted these juicy fruits as war-time treats for the family; all part of the 'grow-it-yourself trend.' Why don't you have a go at growing them yourself? Strawberries have a lot of natural

Strawberry Syrup

sweetness, so do adjust the sugar levels according to your own preferences. In these more prosperous times, strawberry syrup is the perfect addition to desserts, as well as being a really quick and easy way to make a cheats Strawberry Daiquiri… (shhh… we didn't tell you!)

For a truly traditional flair, drink garnished with deck chairs, gingham picnic rugs, *strawberries and cream* and the tennis! Lovely.

Strawberry Syrup

500g Strawberries

150g Sugar (to taste, depending on tartness of strawberries)

200ml Cold Water

Strawberry Syrup

1. Place the strawberries, sugar and water in a heavy-bottomed saucepan and heat gently until the juices flow freely. **2.** Strain the juice through a clean muslin cloth. **3.** Heat the mixture for a further five minutes, skimming any scum which rises to the top. **4.** Allow the mixture to cool slightly, and pour into sterilised bottles before storing.

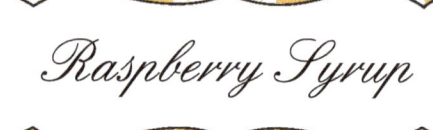

RASPBERRY SYRUP

"That's awfully nice raspberry cordial, Anne,' she said. 'I didn't know raspberry cordial was so nice…"

Lucy Maud Montgomery, Anne of Green Gables, *(1908)*

The brightly coloured juice that you can gather from ripe, fresh raspberries will make this syrup taste as vibrant as it looks. And hopefully unlike poor little Anne of Green Gables, you will not suffer any 'tragic results' with your raspberry cordial. (She had mistaken blackcurrant wine for the cordial, getting her young friend Diana completely drunk - Oh dear!) Just like the strawberries though, Scotland is famous for its raspberry growing and in the late fifties raspberries were taken from

Raspberry Syrup

Scotland to Covent Garden on a steam train known as the 'Raspberry Special.' Now thats How They Used To Do It - in style!

Here is a slightly more complicated Raspberry recipe for a truly delicious syrup. This recipe will be a perfect match to chocolate (especially dark chocolate) desserts, so you may want to make the end-product a bit thicker than usual. The cornflour will help with this, but is entirely optional. Just like the strawberry syrup again, you may serve it straight away (warm, over pancakes or ice-cream is a treat), or freeze it to save for later.

Raspberry Syrup

500g Raspberries (fresh or frozen)
10g Cornflour
100g Sugar
10g Butter
A dash of Water
1 Lemon (to taste)
1 Vanilla Pod (to taste)

Raspberry Syrup

1. Add the water, cornflour, lemon and sugar together in a saucepan – heat and stir until it forms a smooth, runny paste. **2.** Add the raspberries and cook on a low heat until they begin to break down. **3.** It is up to you whether you strain the mixture at this point – to create a smooth syrup. You can alternatively keep the raspberry bits in, for a more full-bodied result. **4.** Take the mixture off the heat, and melt in the butter and the vanilla. **5.** Decant into bottles and jars, and your raspberry syrup is ready to serve.

Blackcurrant and Liquorice Cordial

BLACKCURRANT AND LIQUORICE CORDIAL

For something a bit different…

… Why not try 'Blackcurrant and Liquorice' Cordial?

This recipe uses exactly the same basic technique as the blackberry cordial. Currants are another seasonal fruit which can be found in abundance during Autumn, and great for getting into the 'How They Used To Do It' vibe. If you find yourself with a glut of these delicious little fruits, why not try this simple, and slightly unusual recipe? Blackcurrants are also full of all manner of health promoting antioxidants. Do add more or less sugar than the recipe states, depending on how ripe your currants are. The flavours of Liquorice

Blackcurrant and Liquorice Cordial

should bring childhood memories flooding back. Liquorice is a highly personal ingredient though, so feel free to play around with the amounts (as you would with cinnamon), according to taste.

Try ontop of ice cream, or even as a pork marinade; as any thrifty do-it-yourselfer will testify, cordials are not just for imbibing!

Blackcurrant and Liquorice Cordial

500g Blackcurrants
Natural Liquorice Root (sticks or 'chips' to taste)
250g Caster Sugar
Cold Water (to cover)
1 Lemon

Blackcurrant and Liquorice Cordial

1. De-stalk and wash the blackcurrants. **2.** Place the blackcurrants, liquorice, sugar and water into a medium saucepan, and cook over a low heat, stirring occasionally to help the sugar dissolve. **3.** Once the sugar has dissolved bring the syrup to a gentle simmer. **4.** Simmer the fruits for 5 minutes, and then add the juice and chopped peel of the lemon. **5.** Bring the syrup back to simmer for further 5 minutes. **6.** Strain the liquid through a clean muslin cloth, and let it cool for roughly ten minutes. **7.** You may strain the cordial a second time if you feel it needs it, or alternatively pour the mix straight into your sterilised bottles.

Old Fashioned Fruits

Cordial Counsel: Fruits

"Those syrups that are prepared from fruits should be made with great care.

The fruit should be fully ripe, and freed from all its natural attachments, as stems, leaves, &c., and from all other impurities, without being previously crushed. It should be put into canvas or woollen bags, which should be about two thirds full when placed under the press; the expressing force should be gradually increased so as to effectually remove the juice with as little of the fibre of the fruit as possible.

It is customary to make a pint of syrup from a pint measure of the fruit, and if the expressed juice is insufficient for the purpose, to dilute it with water.

Your fruit should always be prime, and gathered dry, and picked clean from stalks."

Pierre Lacour, The Manufacture of Liquors, Wines, and Cordials, Without the Aid of Distillation *(1863)*

Blood Orange Syrup

BLOOD ORANGE SYRUP

Oranges…

Old-fashioned recipes for orange syrups and cordials tended to utilise 'Bigarade', that is a slightly bitter Seville orange grown throughout the mediterranean region. It had thicker skin and was thus easier to transport on long sea voyages, as well as being high in pectin - perfect for making marmalade. These days, the standard 'sweet orange' has replaced this unusual fruit, but it still makes a perfect ingredient for the home-chef wishing to preserve a glut of seasonal produce. For your perusal, here we have an updated version - 'blood orange syrup' - a modern take on the traditional classic. It is best served with sparkling water (or sparkling wine, dependant

Blood Orange Syrup

on preference!), as its bright-red colour really livens up any drink. The syrup is simple and thirst-quenching, as well as taking no time at all to prepare. It is also easy to make in large batches and thus makes the perfect summer daytime tipple.

If you are lucky enough to have some, and you do wish to make it with the traditional Seville oranges, just use a little more sugar.

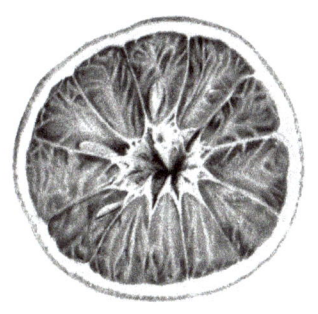

Blood Orange Syrup

150ml of Blood Orange Juice / Pink Grapefruit Juice

100g Sugar (more if using Grapefruits)

A teaspoon of Orange Zest

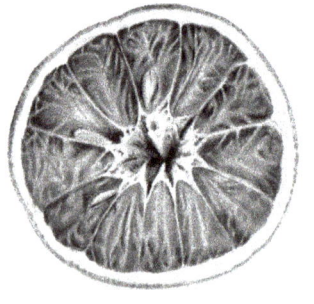

Blood Orange Syrup

1. Add the juice and sugar to a saucepan, and cook until the sugar has completely dissolved. **2.** Now take it off the heat, add the zest from the oranges, and allow to cool. **3.** Strain through a clean piece of muslin, and then decant into sterilised jars or bottles. **4.** Your *Citrus Sparkler* is ready to serve!

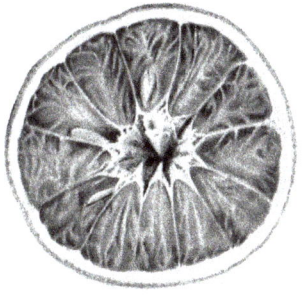

Plum Syrup

PLUM SYRUP

Plums are particularly good fruits for syrup-making, found in abundance in England during the autumn months. If you are lucky enough to get a glut of these delicious little fruits, making plum syrup is the perfect way to preserve the juices of these fruits to enjoy at a later date.

Although in most supermarkets you will find mostly foreign plums, this most certainly would not have been 'How They Used To Do it!' Transporting fruit-en masse simply did not take place until relatively recently. British plums are in fact some of the best you can get, so picking them yourself is an added bonus. When they are at their ripest, British plums have a tender, satin-like skin, with a delicate white 'bloom' around them, which rubs off when the fruit is handled. The flesh inside is mellow and satisfying.

Plum Syrup

A perfect ingredient for this little cook-book, plums are gorgeous in pies, crumbles, tarts and jams – as well as a surprisingly good addition to salad dressings or simple tomato salads. Your syrup will give added depth and flavour to all of these dishes – not to mention a pleasant accompaniment to savoury meals such as roast pork. As a final thought… Nectarines are just as wonderful to use, although they will generally have to be shop bought. The *combination* of plum *and* nectarine is a fantastic one too, so why not try replacing half the plums with nectarines, for a truly exciting syrup?

Plum Syrup

500g Plums
150g Sugar (to taste)
Water (to cover)

Plum Syrup

1. Fill a sterilised jar 2/3 full with ripe plums including the stones. Stand the jar in a saucepan of boiling water and simmer until the fruit is soft and the juice flows freely. **2.** Strain the liquid through a clean muslin cloth. **3.** Combine the juice and the sugar in a saucepan– (making sure to taste when adding the sugar). **4.** Boil the mixture for approximately fifteen minutes, skimming any scum. **5.** Allow to cool, and pour into sterilised bottles before storing. **6.** Serve as a drink, with sparkling water – or serve as a dessert over waffles, ice-cream, cakes – or any other combination.

Pineapple Syrup

PINEAPPLE SYRUP

"This can be made in the same manner as blackberry, or by slicing the fruit, alternating the slices with layers of powdered sugar, permitting them to stand twenty-four hours, and then expressing the syrup formed. Each pound of the prepared fruit, with thirty ounces of sugar, should yield, with the requisite quantity of water, two pints of syrup.

This syrup will have its aromatic aroma greatly impaired by heat."

Pineapples have been used in English kitchens for longer than you might think! There is infact a painting, created in 1675 by Hendrik Danckerts, which depicts Charles II being

Pineapple Syrup

presented with the first pineapple grown in England. Whilst this exotic fruit would have been a substantial luxury for the average family, even in the early years of the twentieth century, there are records of pineapple being used. Because of their rarity, finding novel ways to preserve this delicious fruit was even more important!

This recipe for pineapple syrup makes a wonderfully sweet and sticky juice which is perfect to stock in your kitchen for the summer months. It will give a tropical flair to any dish – sweet or savoury. Mixed with other cordials, or simply sparkling water this is the perfect summer tipple.

Pineapple Syrup

500g peeled, sliced Pineapple
100ml Water
100g Sugar

Pineapple Syrup

1. Crush the fruit in a large jar and pour the water over it. **2.** Stand the jar in a pan of boiling water and cook gently for two hours until the fruit is tender. **3.** Strain the liquid through a clean muslin cloth, and add the sugar to taste. **4.** Put the mixture into a saucepan, bring to the boil again and cook for a further fifteen minutes, skimming any scum. **5.** Allow to cool, then carefully pour into sterilised bottles to store. Voila.

APRICOCK SYRUP

For something a bit different…

… Why not try 'Apricock Syrup'?

"Take three pounds of sugar, and three quarts of water; let them boil together and skim it well. Then put in six pounds of apricocks, pared and stoned, and let them boil until they are tender; then take them up and when the liquid is cold bottle it up. You may if you please, after you have taken out the apricocks, let the liquid have one boil with a sprig of flowered clary in it; the apricocks make marmalade, and are very good for preserves."

Apricock Syrup

Apricots are a lovely little fruit, a favourite of the Victorian art critic John Ruskin, who described them as 'shining [fruit] in a sweet brightness of golden velvet.' They also used to be called, 'Apricocks'! England is not famed for growing fantastic apricots, however it has happened on a small scale since the sixteenth century – and when they are right and ripe, there's nothing better. Most of our apricots will come from Spain, France, South Africa or California, and they were not widely available (except to a select few English home growers) until the mid-twentieth century. Henry VIII was probably the first home-grower, when his gardener brought back some apricot trees from Italy. Their naturally sweet, syrupy nature will make apricots the perfect addition to your syrup repertoire though. Add a bit of honey for some old-fashioned sweet roundness; a wonderful combination.

Apricock Syrup

500g fresh apricots, halved and pitted
250g Sugar
1 Lemon
100ml Water

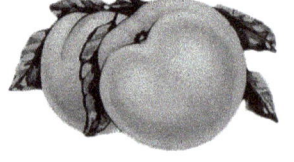

Apricock Syrup

1. Puree about half the apricots and half the water in a blender. **2.** Put this mixture, along with the sugar – a dash of lemon juice (and zest if you like) into a large saucepan. **3.** Add the rest of the apricots and water, and stir over a medium heat until the sugar dissolves and everything comes to the boil. **4.** Stir for a further five minutes. **5.** Allow to cool, and then pour the liquid into your sterilised containers. Your syrup is ready to serve!

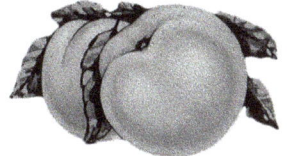

Flowers and Hedgerows

"JUST LIVING IS NOT ENOUGH… ONE MUST HAVE SUNSHINE, FREEDOM, AND A LITTLE FLOWER."

Hans Christian Andersen.

Lavender Syrup

LAVENDER SYRUP

Lavender is a wonderful flower, famed for its aroma as well as its decorative uses. The English word for lavender is generally thought to derive from the Old French *lavandre*, and ultimately from the Latin *lavare* (to wash) – referring to the use of lavender infusions in baths. Today, you will be extremely lucky to have a lavender infused bath, but use it in your home cooking – and experience the same pleasures. It is a great flower for this *How They Used To Do It* collection, mainly for its many and varied uses. Lavender flowers can be candied and are sometimes used as cake decorations, and it is also grown as a condiment, used in salads and dressing. Lavender also yields abundant nectar, from which our much maligned bees can make high quality honey. This plant lends a floral and slightly sweet flavour to most dishes, and is

Lavender Syrup

therefore perfect when paired with sheep's-milk and goat's-milk cheeses. Pair your syrup with chocolate for a truly stunning dessert, or even try it with refreshing iced tea with a honey sweetener. Delicious!

Lavender Syrup

1 tablespoon dried Lavender (or more, fresh, if you're lucky enough to grow it yourself)

225ml Water

100g Sugar

Lavender Syrup

1. Place the water, sugar and lavender in a saucepan, and bring to the boil. **2.** Stir the mixture occasionally, and once at the boil, simmer for a further two minutes. **3.** Strain through a piece of muslin, and leave the liquid to cool. **4.** Place your syrup in some well-sealed containers, and it will keep for at least two weeks in the refrigerator, and longer if frozen.

Rose Syrup

ROSE SYRUP

"What's in a name? That which we call a rose by any other name would smell as sweet."

William Shakespeare.

"Take of dried rose petals, two ounces; infuse the roses in a pint of water for twelve hours; the water should be boiling when the roses are added; after they have infused, strain the liquid, and dissolve two ounces of sugar in it, and proceed as for other syrups."

Roses have a truly heady, delicious scent and in the British summer months, their blooms are everywhere! They are so pretty to look at, but are also great in cooking; used to

Rose Syrup

great extent in Middle Eastern and Indian cuisines. Roses have also been used in English cooking since Tudor times (although they have since fallen out of fashion), but they have such varied uses – as a flavouring for cocktails, to scent honey, make sugared petals for cake decorations, rose petal jams or even in a salad. Roses were originally prized for their medicinal virtues, and rosehips are an especially good source of vitamin C. During the Second World War, this fact proved very useful to the struggling home-population, when citrus was no longer commercially available. As a result of this the British Government encouraged groups of people to roam out into the countryside and gather rosehips from the wild hedgerow to make into syrup. Importantly, this was then shared amongst the local community - boosting morale as well as immune systems! What better reason is there for you to try (this slightly updated) rose-water syrup?

Rose Syrup

100ml Rose Water (or replace with home-grown petals if you have them)

400 ml water

400g sugar

1 Lime

Rose Syrup

1. Bring the water and the sugar to the boil in a large saucepan. **2.** Simmer for ten minutes. **3.** Then add a dash of lime juice (more or less, according to taste) and rose water, and cook for ten minutes longer, stirring occasionally. **4.** Take the pan off the heat and allow to cool. **5.** Pour the syrup into your sterilised bottles, and it is ready to use!

Rose Petals

ROSE PETALS

If you would like to try making some sugared rose petals (they do make a fantastic garnish), here is a classic recipe for your own amusement:

"Dip a rose that is neither in the bud, nor over-blowne, in a sirup, consisting of sugar, double refined, and Rose-water boiled to his full height, then open the leaves one by one with a fine smooth bodkin either of bone or wood; and presently if it be a hot sunny day, and whilest the sunne is in some good height, lay them on papers in the sunne, or else dry them with some gentle heat in a close roome, heating the room before you set them in, or in an oven upon papers, in pewter dishes, and then put them up in glasses; and keepe them in dry cupboards

Rose Petals

neere the fire. You may prove this preserving with sugar-candy instead of sugar if you please."

Sir Hugh Platt, Delights for Ladies *(1594)*

Whilst this may sound complicated – all you really need to do is dip your rose petals in egg whites or a simple syrup, and then place them in some caster sugar. No bone bodkins, close rooms or pewter dishes required!

VIOLET SYRUP

Take fresh violets one pound; boiling water, two pints and a half; infuse the flowers for twenty-four hours in the water, in a covered glass or earthenware vessel, and strain the water from the violets without squeezing, and dissolve six pounds of sugar in the filtered liquor, and proceed as for other syrups. This syrup, when prepared in pewter-lined vessels, is of a beautiful blue colour. This colour will, in the course of time, fade.

Sweet violet syrup is a really simple and impressive thing to make – giving an amazing colour and perfume, sure to impress your guests. Many English gardens in the spring time will be covered with these sweet-smelling violets, and they can also be sugared (just like the rose recipe above) and

Violet Syrup

used for cake or table decorations. Violets have been used in traditional cooking for many years, as when newly open they are lovely decorations for salads or stuffings, and alternatively, soufflés, crea and similar desserts can be flavoured with their essence. Only a very small amount of this syrup is needed in beverages and desserts, because of its strong flavour – but it makes a very sophisticated drink when mixed with sparkling wine or lemonade, garnished with a fresh flower.

Violet Syrup

85 grams of sweet violets (about six handfuls)
300ml boiling water
600g sugar

Violet Syrup

1. Remove all the green, stalks and leaves from the violets and place them in a large saucepan. **2.** Pour over the boiling water, cover with a lid and allow to infuse overnight. **3.** The next day, add the sugar and bring the mixture to a gentle boil, stirring until the sugar has completely dissolved. **4.** Strain the syrup through a muslin cloth, and decant into your sterilised containers.

Lovage Cordial

LOVAGE CORDIAL

For something a bit different….

…. Why not try 'Lovage Cordial'?

Lovage has long been cultivated in Europe, with its leaves used as herbs, the roots as vegetables and the seeds as spices. The sturdy leaves can be used in salads or to season broth, and the flavour is something like parsley and celery, combined with just a hint of aniseed! It is incredibly easy to grow from seed – so why not have a go yourself? It will be a wonderful addition to any kitchen herb garden. Lovage is also famed for its many health benefits; lovage tea can be

Lovage Cordial

applied to wounds as an antiseptic, or drunk to stimulate digestion. It has been admired since the times of the ancient Greeks and romans, and over the centuries it was believed to cure everything from rheumatism to sore throats and smelly feet! It was also famed as an aphrodisiac. In terms of lovage cordial more specifically, *How They Used To Do It* was to mix the leaves with brandy and sugar as a warming winter drink (by all means try it out!). Here, we have a slightly simpler non-alcoholic version for your delectation.

Lovage Cordial

**1 tablespoon dried Lovage
(or more leaves, fresh, if you're lucky enough to grow it yourself)**

225ml Water

100g Sugar

Lovage Cordial

1. Place the water, sugar and lovage leaves in a saucepan, and bring to the boil. **2.** Stir the mixture occasionally, and once at the boil, simmer for a further two minutes. **3.** Strain through a piece of muslin, and leave the liquid to cool. **4.** Place your syrup in some well-sealed containers, and it will keep for at least two weeks in the refrigerator, and longer if frozen.

Sugar and Spice and All Things Nice

Cordial Counsel: Natural Sweetening - Honey

"Owing to its peculiar, though feebly aromatic taste, honey is one of the most useful articles that can be found for giving a fine body…

When used in the finer liquids, it may sometimes need clarifying; but, generally, if it should be heated and strained, will answer all purposes. The usual impurities are earth, sand and colouring.

To Clarify – Gently heating the honey and straining through muslin, will generally remove the impurities; or mix six eggs with two gallons of water, and add the water to ten gallons of honey; mix well, thin, and apply heat, but do not bring it to the boiling point; then skim, and if necessary, strain."

Pierre Lacour, The Manufacture of Liquors, Wines, andCordials, Without the Aid of Distillation *(1863)*

ANISEED CORDIAL

The seed are brought from Spain, Germany and France. The Spanish are smaller than either, and are usually preferred. The seed appear of a light greenish brown colour, with a shade of yellow; their odour is increased by friction, and is too well known to need a description; their taste is warm, sweet and aromatic.

The distinctive taste of aniseed, from the anise flower, is the perfect ingredient to use in a cordial. You will only need a little, as the aniseed flavour really comes through in this drink. Diluted with a little water, this makes a wonderful

Aniseed Cordial

alcohol-free aperitif, much like the traditional French beverage, Pastis. Enjoy as a refreshing mid-day drink, or as a before-dinner palate cleanser!

Did you know… In 1305, King Edward I of England placed a tax on aniseed. Famed for helping with digestion, it was in great demand - such was its popularity, that the revenue earned through its import helped repair damages to *Old London Bridge*.

Aniseed Cordial

30g Aniseed
225g Sugar
1 litre of Water

Aniseed Cordial

1. This is such a simple recipe to make: In a heavy-bottomed saucepan, gently heat all the ingredients until the sugar has dissolved. This should take about ten minutes. **2.** Strain the liquid through a clean muslin cloth. **3.** Pour into sterilised bottles to store – and keep in the fridge or freezer.

Cinnamon Cordial

CINNAMON CORDIAL

"This odour has become too popular with the masses to be of any value to the manufacturer. Cinnamon is the flavouring ingredient in some aromatic cordials; when it is used it should be concealed to as great an extent as possible. Cinnamon is highly useful where a warm aromatic odor is required."

Cinnamon is a wonderfully evocative spice, and is found in many foodstuffs and beverages especially in winter and during the festive season. Its flavour is the result of an essential oil that makes up roughly 0.5 - 1% of its composition, but 99% of the taste. This cordial is the perfect tipple to offer Christmas guests who would rather enjoy something alcohol-free, and is also delicious added to coffee or hot chocolate for

Cinnamon Cordial

a warming winter treat. You could also try it alongside some christmas cinnamon cookies... a sure way to impress your festive guests!

Cinnamon Cordial

150g Bruised Cinnamon Sticks
200g Sugar
900ml Warm Water

Cinnamon Cordial

1. Place the ingredients into a sterilised jar and shake thoroughly. It is important at this stage to use warm water, instead of boiling water – otherwise the nuanced flavour of the cinnamon sticks will be lost. **2.** Leave this mixture to stand for ten days, but return once a day to thoroughly shake the ingredients. **3.** After the ten days are up, carefully filter the liquid through a clean muslin cloth, and into sterilised bottles to store.

Juniper Cordial

JUNIPER CORDIAL

"Patience is bitter, but its fruit is sweet."

Jean-Jacques Rousseau

"The berries, as the fruit is sometimes called, are sometimes collected in this country; but though equal to the European in appearance, they are inferior in strength, and are not much used. The best comes from Europe, particularly from Trieste and the Italian ports. They are globular, more or less shrivelled, about as large as a pea, covered with a glaucous bloom, beneath which they are of a shining, blackish purple colour, and containing a brownish yellow pulp and three angular seeds."

Juniper Cordial

Juniper berries are the base ingredients in gin, giving the spirit its distinctive taste and aroma. As an interesting aside; the juniper berry is not in actual fact a true berry; rather it is a cone with unusually fleshy and merged scales, which give it a berry-like appearance. It is grown all over the northern hemisphere, and is particularly famed in Scotland, where traditionally at Hogmanay (New Year), the smoke of burning juniper is used to cleanse, bless and protect the household and its inhabitants. This recipe for juniper cordial is wonderfully simple to make at home, and has the added accent of coriander, too. You will notice it contains less fruit than most of the other recipes; this is because of the wonderful, strong flavour that juniper's possess. Try mixing it with tonic water and a squeeze of lime for a delicious alcohol-free gin and tonic...

Juniper Cordial

15g dried Juniper Berries
225ml Water
One bunch of Coriander
225ml Sugar Syrup

Juniper Cordial

1. Crush the juniper berries in a large (sterilised) jar, and add the water. **2.** Add the coriander and sugar syrup and shake well. **3.** Allow the mixture to stand for two weeks (no cheating!) then carefully strain the liquid through a clean muslin cloth. **4.** Pour into sterilised bottles to store.

CLOVE CORDIAL

For something a little different…

…. Why not try 'Clove Cordial'?

Cloves are the wonderfully aromatic flower buds of a tree native to Indonesia. Whilst the spice has been used in Asian, African and Middle Eastern cooking for a very long time, it only came to Europe in the seventeenth century – once the spice trading routes had been opened up. Once cloves had arrived however, they became a staple with many British families, now adorning meats and onions (think Christmas bread sauce) as well as complementing fruits such as apples, pears or rhubarb. About 85% of a cloves' powerful taste is

Clove Cordial

imparted by the chemical 'eugenol', and so the quantity of spice required is typically relatively small. This makes it the perfect flavouring for thrifty, do-it-yourself recipes; producing big flavour for little cost. Cloves also pair well with cinnamon, allspice, vanilla, basil, citrus peel, star anise or peppercorns – so do feel free to experiment!

This recipe uses exactly the same method (though a few extra ingredients) as the cinnamon cordial, do add extras or take some away according to taste.

Clove Cordial

2 Oranges (just the peel)
2 Cinnamon Sticks
8 Cloves
300g Sugar
900ml Warm Water

Clove Cordial

1. Place *all* the ingredients into a sterilised jar and shake thoroughly. It is important at this stage to use warm water, instead of boiling water – otherwise the nuanced flavour of the spices and peel will be lost.
2. Leave this mixture to stand for ten days, but return once a day to thoroughly shake the ingredients.
3. After the ten days are up, carefully filter the liquid through a clean muslin cloth, and into sterilised bottles to store. Your cordial is ready to serve!

Medicinal and Herbal Cordials

"THE FRUIT OF YOUR OWN HARD WORK IS THE SWEETEST."

Deepika Padukone

Cranberry Syrup

CRANBERRY SYRUP

Another festive recipe is this one, which uses the rich, ruby-red fruit; cranberries. Most widely used and grown in North America, cranberries are a fantastic little berry, rich in vitamins C, D, potassium and iron. They are also believed to be a natural remedy for a whole host of health conditions. Cranberries really do come into their own around Christmas, and no hostess's cupboard would be complete without some homemade cranberry sauce. They are good for much more than merely accompanying the turkey though, and you can use your syrup in both sweet and savoury dishes (as well as drinks of course). As cranberries can be quite tart and sour,

Cranberry Syrup

especially when under ripe, do feel free to add more sugar to this syrup to taste. This will make a thoroughly refreshing beverage on its own, although why not experiment mixing it with the cinnamon cordial for a truly Christmassy taste?

Cranberry Syrup

500g ripe Cranberries
Boiling Water (to cover)
200g Sugar for every 200ml of juice produced.

Cranberry Syrup

1. Place the fruit in a pan of boiling water and simmer gently for two hours. In order to keep the moisture in, place a slightly smaller pan lid over the fruit. **2.** Strain the resulting liquid through a clean muslin cloth, measure carefully and add the sugar. **3.** Bring to the boil again and skim off any scum which comes to the surface. **4.** Leave to cool, and pour into sterilised bottles before storing.

Dandelion Cordial

"Are you separated from the object of your love? Carefully pluck one of the feathery heads; charge each of the little feathers composing it with a tender thought; turn towards the spot where the loved one dwells; blow, and the seed-ball will convey your message faithfully. Do you wish to know if that dear one is thinking of you? blow again; and if there be left upon the stalk a single aigrette, it is a proof you are not forgotten. Similarly, the dandelion is consulted as to whether the lover lives east, west, north, or south, and whether he is coming or not."

Alexander F. Chamberlain,
The Child and Childhood in Folk-Thought *(1896)*

Dandelion Cordial

Aside from this lovely folk-belief, today dandelions are thought to be very good for the body, and rather easy to make into a delicious cordial to boot! One of the main benefits of dandelions is that they are very good for the liver. The antioxidants like vitamin-C and Luteolin can keep the liver functioning in optimal gear and protect it from aging. This is a great cordial to make, as Dandelions appear in almost every garden around Britain, allowing for a bit of home-foraging! For a true timeless classic, why not try mixing the dandelion with burdock? Such drinks have been consumed in the British isles since the thirteenth century - all the way to the present day. The mellow burdock should invoke a nostalgic sense of times gone by… Try this subtly flavoured cordial diluted with a little water.

Dandelion Cordial

100g (or slightly more) Dandelion Heads - and the same of burdock roots, if you can get them!

650ml Water

450g Sugar

2 Oranges

2 Lemons

A handful of Raisins

Dandelion Cordial

1. Place the dandelions in a large bowl and cover with the boiling water. **2.** Allow this mixture to stand for three days, then filter through a clean muslin cloth. **3.** Place the liquid in a sterilised bottle with the dissolved sugar, and strained juice of the lemons and oranges. **4.** Allow this mixture to stand for at least three days. **5.** Decant into smaller bottles to store and (if you like), place two raisins in each bottle before sealing. This will impart a rounder, sweeter flavour.

Ginger Syrup

GINGER SYRUP

The warm and spicy flavour of fresh ginger makes a wonderful syrup, and is a very versatile ingredient to have stocked in your drinks cupboard. From its origin to the present, ginger is the world's most widely cultivated herb, but sadly, not as appreciated as it should be! Testimonials of both the medicinal and economic importance of ginger have been recorded as far back as five thousand-year-old Greek literature to 200 B.C.

Try this simple recipe for ginger syrup, which once made, can be added to an array of drinks and cocktails to really spice them up. Unlike most of the other recipes, you will not

Ginger Syrup

need that much ginger here, as the flavour is naturally very strong. Added to hot water and lemon, a little ginger syrup is a great natural remedy for sore throats and colds.

Ginger Syrup

250g Bruised Ginger
1 Lemon
750g Sugar
1.5 litres of Water

Ginger Syrup

1. Cook the ginger and the water in a saucepan, gently simmering for about half an hour. **2.** Add the lemon juice and the sugar and cook for a further fifteen minutes until the sugar has completely dissolved. **3.** Strain the liquid through a muslin cloth and pour into sterilised bottles. **4.** Seal the bottles and store in the fridge or freezer, ready for use.

ROSEHIP CORDIAL

"The quietest of cordials… 'Sub Rosa' literally translates as 'under the rose.' Traditionally, any matters discussed under a rose were to be kept in the strictest confidence. This is why you will often see roses sculpted into the ceilings of old banqueting halls… what was spoken 'sub rosa', and perhaps more pertinently, under the effects of wine was not to be repeated!"

Rosehip is also the perfect pick-me-up cordial for colds and flu. Simply dilute with hot water and honey for an incredibly vitamin-rich, and comforting drink. Rosehips are also reportedly helpful to those suffering from arthritis as it contains polyphenols and anthocyanins, which are believed to ease joint inflammation and prevent joint damage. It's also

Rosehip Cordial

rich in vitamin C, which has antioxidant properties. Aside from its many medicinal properties, Rosehip is also a very traditional english cordial, used in the Second World War, when due to rationing, vitamin C was in short supply. The government actively encouraged groups of villagers to source out these wonderful little flowers in the hedgerows, and share them amongst friends. A far cry from its 'silent' beginnings!

Note that the 'hips' should not be picked until after the first frost, which softens and sweetens them. This cordial would also be wonderful with another English classic - rhubarb (first sold in London by a Mr Joseph Myatt in 1808). Add water or lemonade for a refreshing day-time drink.

Rosehip Cordial

500g Wild Rosehips
200g Caster Sugar
2 Litres of boiling water.

Rosehip Cordial

1. Put the rosehips (and rhubarb if you've got it) in a large saucepan and pour over two litres of boiling water. **2.** Bring the water back to the boil then turn off the heat and allow the rosehips to infuse for fifteen minutes. **3.** Strain the mixture through a clean piece of muslin, squeezing out as much liquid as you can. **4.** Tip the pulp back into the pan, pour over 1.5 litres of water and bring to the boil. Repeat the straining process one more time. Throw away the pulp left in the muslin. **5.** Pour the strained liquid into a clean pan and boil until reduced to one litre. **6.** Skim off any scum that comes to the surface, then stir in the sugar until dissolved. **7.** Allow to cool slightly, and then pour the cordial into sterilised bottles, ready to serve.

Serving Suggestions

Serving Suggestions

There are so many ways to serve cordials and syrups, and hopefully we have given you some ideas with each recipe. The great thing about cordials and syrups, is that they can be paired with savoury or sweet foods alike - think quince with cheese, blackberries with pork (instead of the standard apple sauce), cranberry with stuffing, raspberry with chocolate, elderflower with rhubarb and violets with delicate desserts. The list goes on! Try to think of the fruit or flavouring on its own, and what foods you would pair that with normally – and then exactly the same will apply to your cordial or syrup! For the beginners, try experimenting by using a new flavour of cordial in a tried and tested recipe. Half the fun is in the trialling, so be brave…

Serving Suggestions

Serving Suggestions

Having said this, the classic way to enjoy cordials and syrups is as a beverage; either concentrated, and drank over ice, or as a long drink – either simply with water, or with sparkling lemonade, wine, or even champagne! Here are some handy hints of how to use yours…

Serve cordials as an after dinner aperitif (as already noted, Quince would go fantastically with your cheese course). On their own, the sweetness of cordials will be a lovely, non-alcoholic replacement for dessert wines.

How about sipping slightly chilled cordials from small, stemmed glasses. Take a look in a vintage store and you'll probably find some rather beautifully decorated examples of these small glasses. Over ice is best.

Serving Suggestions

If you wish to get the most out of your cordials' aroma (think of the recipes in the *Sugar and Spice and All things Nice*, and *Flowers and Hedgerows* section), drink them out of a wide brandy glass to better enjoy the wonderful smells. Here, room temperature is best, as it allows the aromas to come through more.

Why not try making a 'cordial frappe'? The same way you would make a coffee frappe – just mix the cordial with ice in a blender. This will create a truly refreshing drink on a hot summers day.

You didn't hear it from us.... But they are also great when mixed as cocktails!

Gorgeous Gifts

Gorgeous Gifts

As we said in the introduction to this little book, the wonderful thing about making your own homemade products is the fun one can have with creating customised labels and garnishes to the finished bottles (think berries, citrus zest, herb sprigs). For the flower cordials, a few fresh flowers are beautiful accompaniments, and this applies for the berries, fruits and spices. Whatever main ingredient you have used, save some back for decoration afterwards. Cordials and syrups really do make the perfect vintage-inspired present as well as personal treat.

Make sure to source some lovely glass bottles (kilner 'clip tops' are probably the best, and most classic example,

Gorgeous Gifts

although you can find similar products in many homeware stores). This will instantly make your beverages look the part! At this point, you can also make your own tags (think brown card and twine) to hang from the bottlenecks, as well as handwritten labels to adorn the your containers. You could also place a little square of material ('gingham' is always lovely, though 'paisley' would also look a treat) over the top of your bottle. Tied with some twine, this gives a great vintage-inspired twist to your presents, and we're sure the recipients will be touched by your efforts.

Ten Top Tricks and Tips

1. Get your utensils and equipment ready before starting.

2. Make time to make cordials regularly, so you always have a supply of ready-to-drink beverages stocked at home.

3. To prevent your cordials fermenting whilst they are in storage, stand the bottles in a saucepan of water on a thick pad of newspaper, with the water up to the necks of the bottles, and bring the water slowly to the boil and boil for five minutes.

4. Make sure you store your creations in sterilised bottles.

5. Sterilisation is easy, simply wash the bottles in very hot soapy water and place them into an oven on the lowest setting for twenty minutes.

6. Be sure to use your sterilised bottles while they are still warm.

Ten Top Tricks and Tips

7. Store your cordials in the fridge or freezer to lengthen their shelf life.

8. Experiment with mixing your cordials to make new variations.

9. Decant your cordials into pretty bottles with handwritten labels for a thoughtful gift.

10. Experiment with sugar free recipes for a healthy teeth-friendly cordial children will love. Always remember to taste as-you-go when adding sugar; as the natural tartness of the fruit will vary.

But most importantly, have fun!

Credits and Attributions

Cover Image, Title page and Page 4 - This work is a derivative of "1956-Electrolux" is copyright © October 17, 2009 James Vaughn, x-ray delta one, made available on Flickr under Creative Commons Attribution 2.0 Generic (CC BY 2.0) http://www.flickr.com/photos/x-ray_delta_ one/4017899831/sizes/l/in/faves-90808113@N04/

Page 30 - This work is a derivative of "It's All You Need" is Copyright © 1950 Posted by noluck_ boston, made available on vintage-ads.livejournal.com http://vintage-ads.livejournal.com/tag/cleaning

Page 36 - This work is a derivative of "LIFE Dec 12, 1955 hamilton watches christmas spread" is Copyright © 1955, posted by Jocelmeow, made available on vintage-ads.livejournal.com http://vintage-ads.livejournal.com/tag/1945

Page 39 - This work is a derivative of "Maxwell House Coffee (1950) " is Copyright © 1950 posted by, pikkewyntjie made available on vintage-ads.livejournal.com http://vintage-ads.livejournal. com/tag/1950

Page 180 - This work is a derivative of "Tiffany Blue" is Copyright © May 18, 2008, Jill Clardy, made available on flickr under Creative commons Attribution 2.0 Generic (CC BY 2.0) http://www.flickr.com/photos/jillclardy/2523850043/

Page 181 - This work is a derivative of "UH-OH - Oreo / Nabisco, 1951" is Copyright © 1951, posted by Man Writing Slash (write_light), made available on vintage-ads.livejournal.com http://vintage-ads.livejournal.com/tag/1919

www.ingramcontent.com/pod-product-compliance
Lightning Source LLC
Chambersburg PA
CBHW040253170426
43191CB00019B/2395